Book of
VICTORIAN ALPHABETS & DESIGNS

Book of
VICTORIAN
ALPHABETS
& DESIGNS

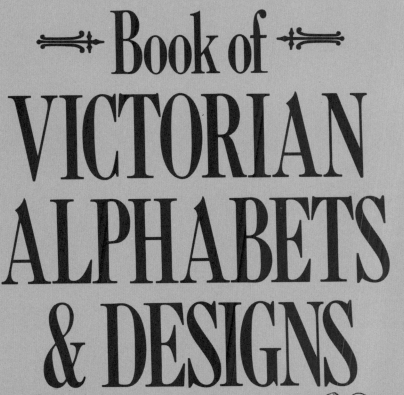

Original Artwork, Free for All To Use

GRAPHIC
ARTS
ARCHIVES
GAA

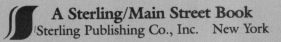

A Sterling/Main Street Book
Sterling Publishing Co., Inc.   New York

10 9 8 7 6 5 4 3 2

A Sterling / Main Street Book

Published in 1990 by Sterling Publishing Company, Inc.
387 Park Avenue South, New York, N.Y. 10016
Originally titled *A Book of Ornamental Alphabets,*
Initials, Monograms and Other Designs
Foreword copyright © 1976 by The Main Street Press
Distributed in Canada by Sterling Publishing
% Canadian Manda Group, P.O. Box 920, Station U
Toronto, Ontario, Canada M8Z 5P9
Distributed in Great Britain and Europe by Cassell PLC
Artillery House, Artillery Row, London SW1P 1RT, England
Distributed in Australia by Capricorn Ltd.
P.O. Box 665, Lane Cove, NSW 2066
Manufactured in the United States of America

ISBN 0-8069-7340-4

Contents

Foreword

Ornament becomes valuable when it is used to add beauty to common things, and to relieve the blankness of bare walls, floors, and ceilings.

—W. Smith Williams, 1863

W. Smith Williams, one of the many contributors to *The Universal Decorator*, published in London in 1863, might have added to his list of drab surfaces those of books, circulars, advertisements, and other printed material. For in his day, as in the present, there was little allowance for public display of the fanciful, the eccentric, the beautiful. At the same time, industrial and commercial artists, experts in graphics among them, were seeking an antidote to the sterility of the Industrial Revolution in a return to the Gothic and earlier styles. "The conclusion is that, amid the din of our lathes and spinning jennies and shuttles, we had better turn to our friends of the olden time for instruction in those arts which embellish the palaces of the affluent, and act no mean part in beguiling the stern realities of indigence." Pre-Raphaelites, followers of John Ruskin, they gave voice to their aesthetic concerns in *The Universal Decorator*, a two-volume handbook from which the 120 plates of *A Book of Ornamental Alphabets, Initials, Monograms, and Other Designs* have been gathered. The original illustrations were drawn by William Gibbs.

The full title of the mid-Victorian work is as lavish and colorful as the plates themselves: *The Universal Decorator, A Complete Guide to Ornamental Design, Designs for Cabinet Makers, Wood Carvers, Metal Workers, Birmingham, Sheffield, and the Potteries—Scrolls, Panels, and General Ornament, Alphabets, Initials, and Monograms.*

Today this artwork has a new meaning. Cranky, fusty, individualistic, it is the antithesis of all that is cheap, quick, and common. The illuminated letters, monograms, and ciphers are particularly eccentric. Yet, in the words of an 1860 commentator, describing medieval book illumination, "The general consistency of the design is so complete, the whole arrangement so continuous—the ornaments appear so truly suggested by the purpose, and so depending on and growing out of each other—that they seem to possess 'a nature' of their own." These letters are probably the most abstruse designs presented in *A Book of Ornamental Alphabets*. . . . It is important to remember, again in the words of our Victorian brethren, that "the free invention of the monks was never trammelled by the necessity of using a character intelligible at once to the ignorant public."

Equally interesting are the designs for panels, frets, bosses, encaustic tiles, centerpieces, guilloches, ribbons and scrolls, trefoils and spandrils—all basic elements in the visual vocabulary of Victorian Gothic design. The twenty-one designs for encaustic, meaning oven-fired, tiles are especially intriguing. Tiles carrying designs of this sort were introduced in England by Herbert Minton, a potter, in the early years of the

Gothic Revival. Rediscovered in the floors of medieval churches and palaces in England and Normandy, they were gradually accepted in the homes of the wealthy and the new public edifices of the mid-Victorian period in North America and Great Britain. Encaustic tiles, in their Minton reincarnation, became terribly fashionable.

Today it is difficult to find such tilework. Most of the Victorian buildings they have graced have since died under the wrecker's ball. The designs, however, refuse to die away altogether. Museum curators, at least, protect from the present such fragments of the past for the future. And books remain, however dusty, as important repositories of ideas and forms which were "antique" yesterday and are suddenly "relevant" today. Let *A Book of Ornamental Alphabets* . . . serve the same useful purpose. The designs are all members of that happy domain called "public." They may be copied freely and frequently without begging anyone's permission. They have been printed on a paper suitable for purposes of reproduction.

Roman Ornamental Alphabet

abcdef

ghiklm

nopqrs

tuvwxyz

Alphabet of the Fifteenth Century

Elizabethan Alphabet

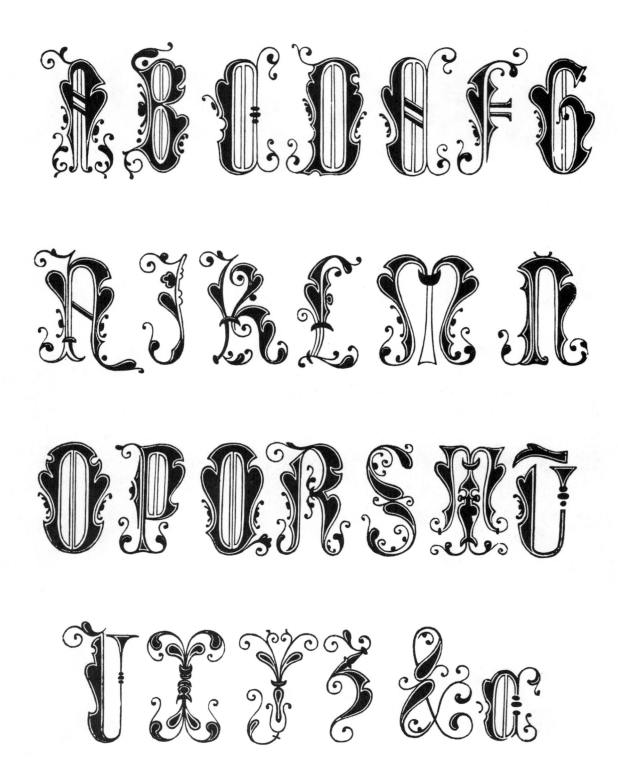

Italian Alphabet of the Sixteenth Century

Gothic Alphabet

ABCDE
FGHIK
LMNO P
RSTU
WXYZ

Alphabet of the Thirteenth Century

abcdef

ghiklm

nopqrs

tvwxyz

Church Text

German Alphabet of the Eleventh Century

abcdefg
hijklmn
opqrstu
vwxyz&

Old English Alphabet

A B C D E
F G H I K
L M N O P
Q R S T U
V W X Y Z

Old English Alphabet

Italian Alphabet of the Thirteenth Century

Alphabet of the Twelfth Century

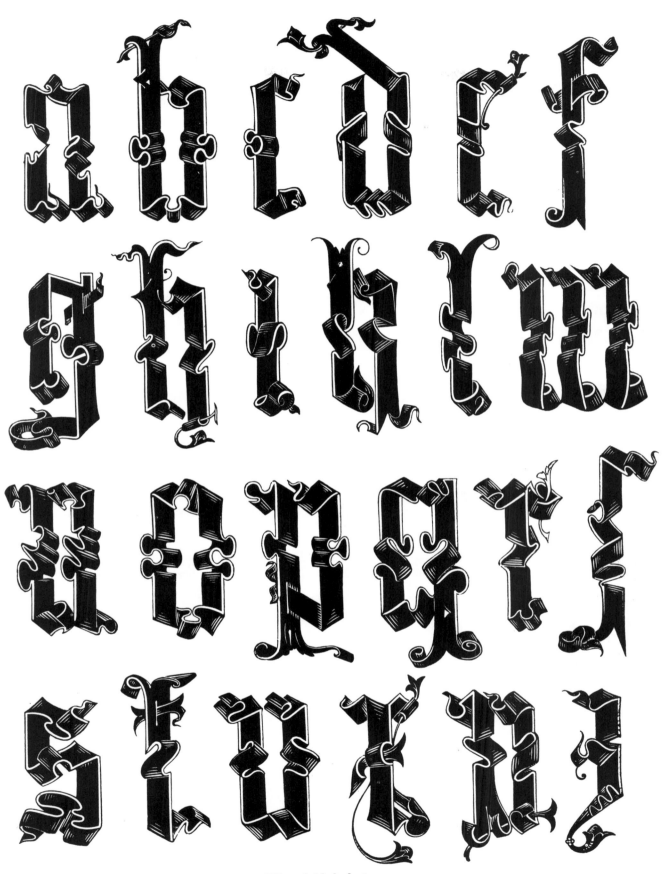

Riband Alphabet

Riband Alphabet

Initial Letters

Initial Letters

Initial Letters

Initial Letters

Initial Letters

Initial Letters

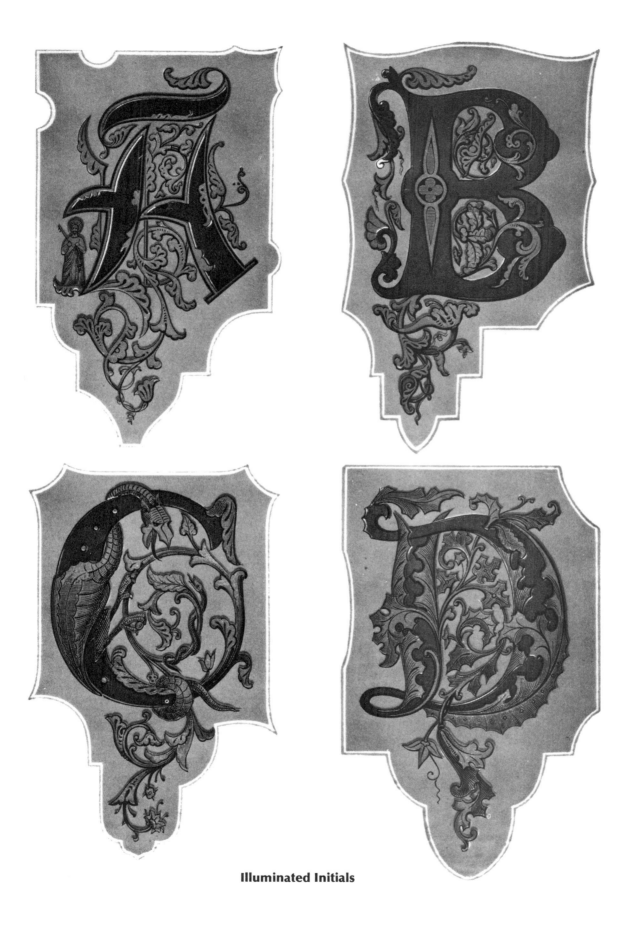

Illuminated Initials

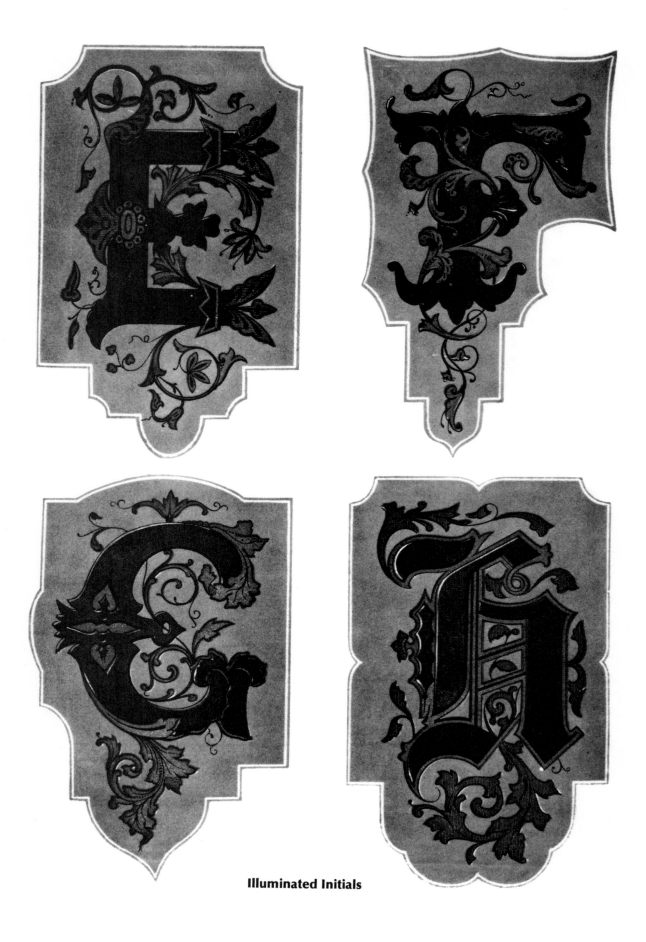

Illuminated Initials

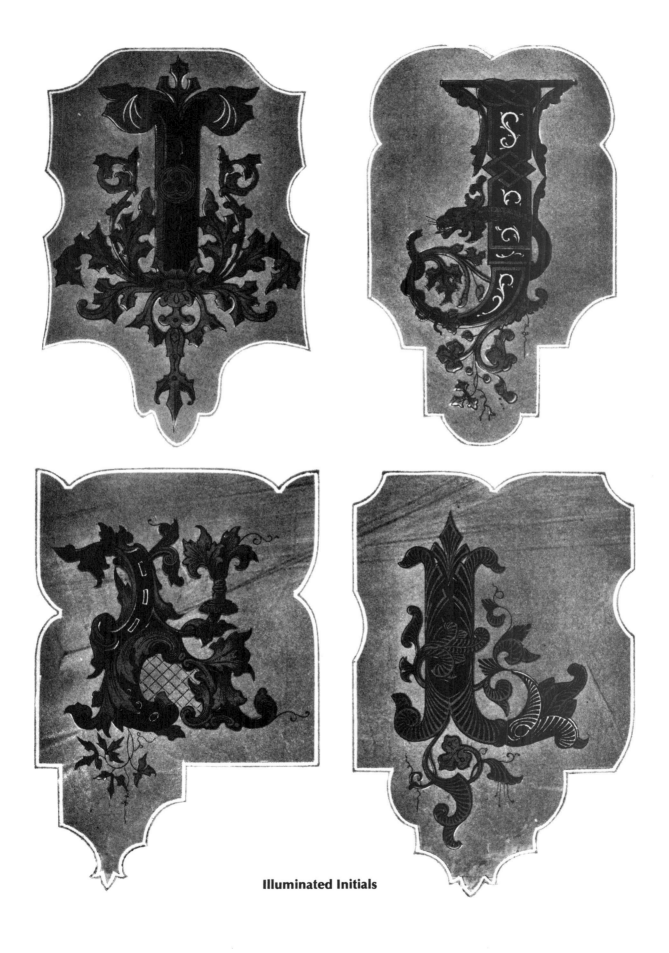

Illuminated Initials

Illuminated Initials

Illuminated Initials

Illuminated Initials

Monograms: JCK, JPN, IHS, AT, SM, ISN

Monograms: PF, TFP, ISM, SAT,WW, EARH

Cyphers: AB, EW, SG, FC

Cyphers and Monograms

Monograms: WHO and SST; Cyphers: TBE and HH

Panel

Panel

Panel

Panel

Panels

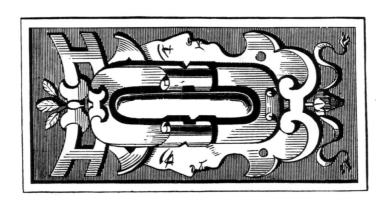

Antique Cabinet Panels, Sixteenth Century

Arabesque Door Panels 1540

Elizabethan Panel

Elizabethan Panels

Elizabethan Panels

French Panel

Greek Panel

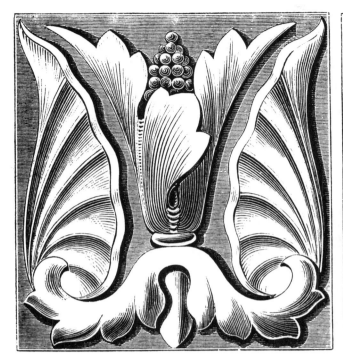

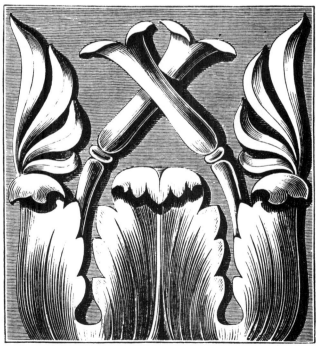

Greek Panels

Italian Panel

Italian Panel

Italian Panel

Renaissance Panel

Renaissance Panels

Design for a Frieze

Byzantine Friezes

Gothic Friezes

Greek Friezes

Greek Friezes

Italian Design for Buhlwork

Italian Frieze

Italian Friezes

Roman Frieze

Arabesque Capitals

Composite Capital

Corinthian Capital

Acanthus Mollis, The Supposed Origin of the Corinthian Capital

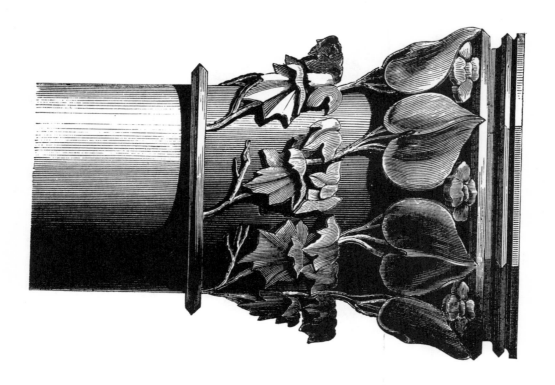

Gothic Capitals

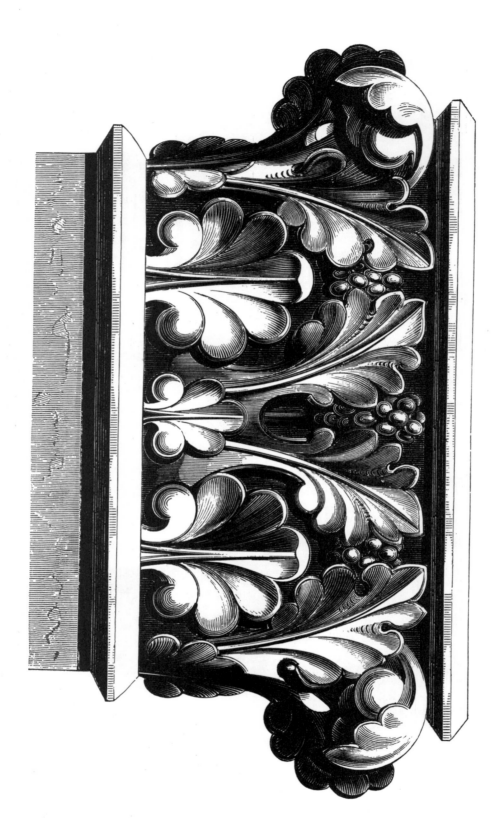

Capital for Gothic Pilaster

Gothic Capital From the Church of St. Clotilde, Paris

Roman Doric

Roman Ionic

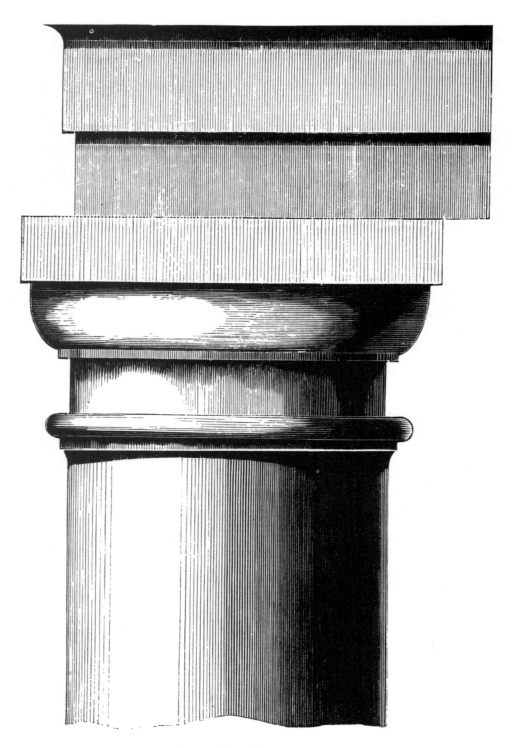

Tuscan Capital

Borders

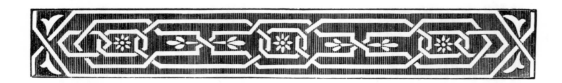

Alhambra Borders

Etruscan Borders

Etruscan Borders

French Borders

Germanesque Borders

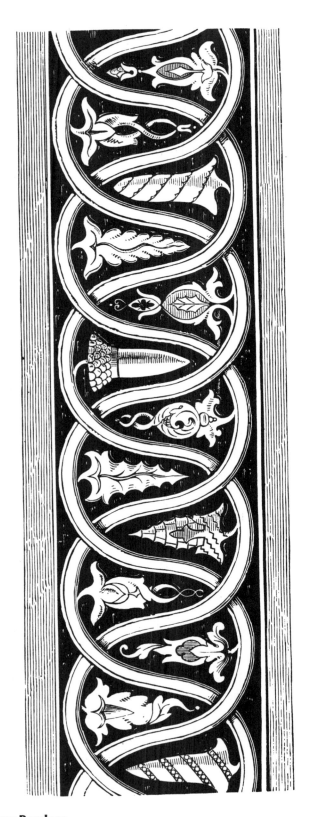

Germanesque Borders

Germanesque Borders

Border, Corner, and Centre

Arabesque Centrepiece

Elizabethan Centrepiece

Greek Centrepiece

Greek Centrepiece

Greek Centrepiece

Greek Centrepieces

Gothic and Arabesque Corners

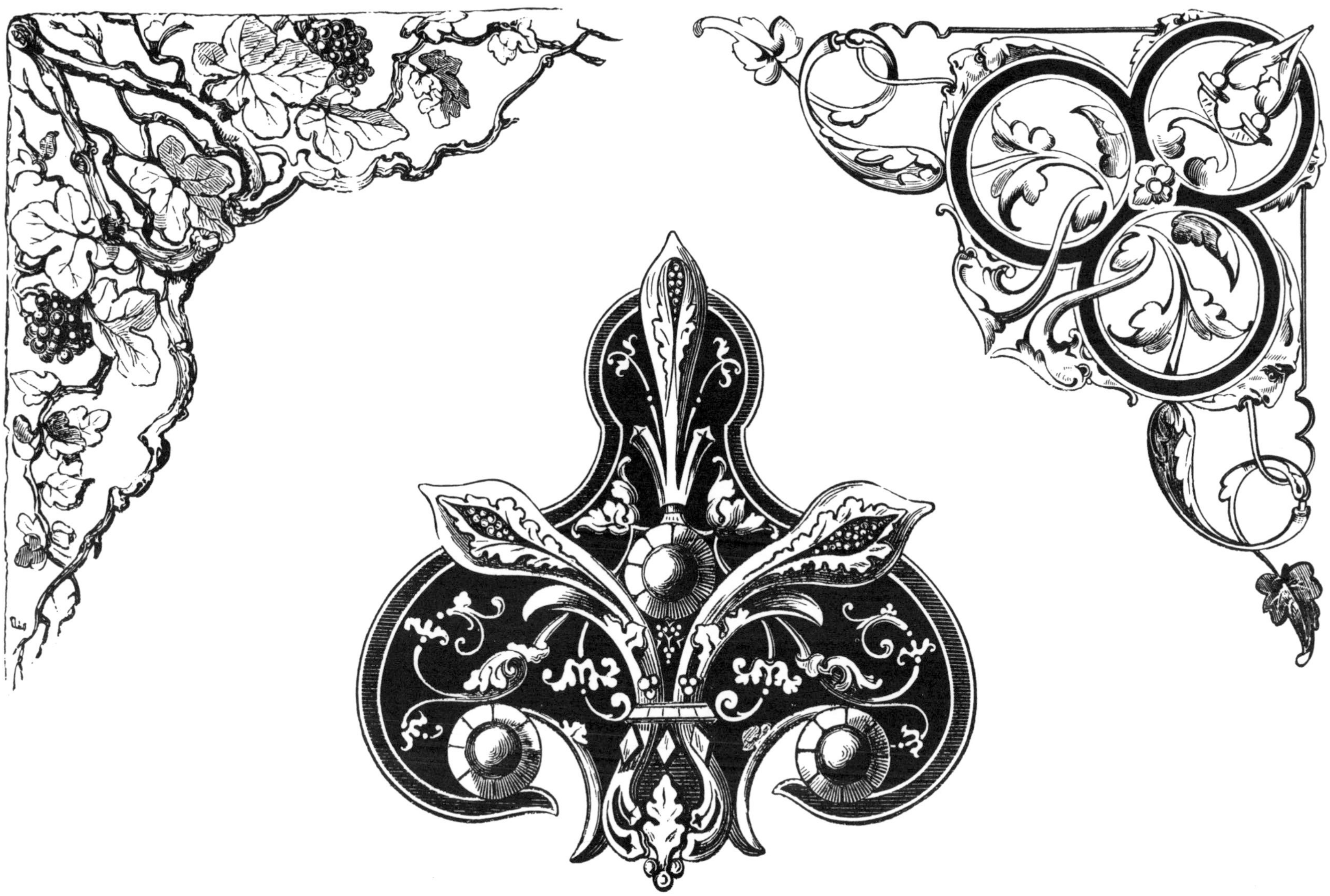

Corners and Centrepiece

Corners and Centrepieces

Arabesque Corner and Centre

Arabesque Centre and Italian Corners

Elizabethan Corners and Centrepiece

German Corner and Centrepiece

Frets

Encaustic Tiles

Encaustic Tiles

Encaustic Tiles

Tessellated Pavements

Alhambra Mosaic

Guilloches

Guilloches

Greek Boss

Greek and Gothic Bosses

Gothic Bosses or Knots

Gothic Crockets and Boss

Gothic Rosette

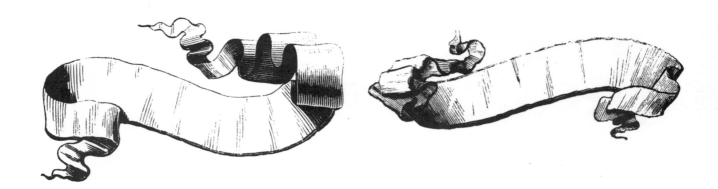

Ribbons

Scroll

Louis XIV Scrolls

Early English Gothic Spandril

Early English Gothic Spandril

Gothic Spandril

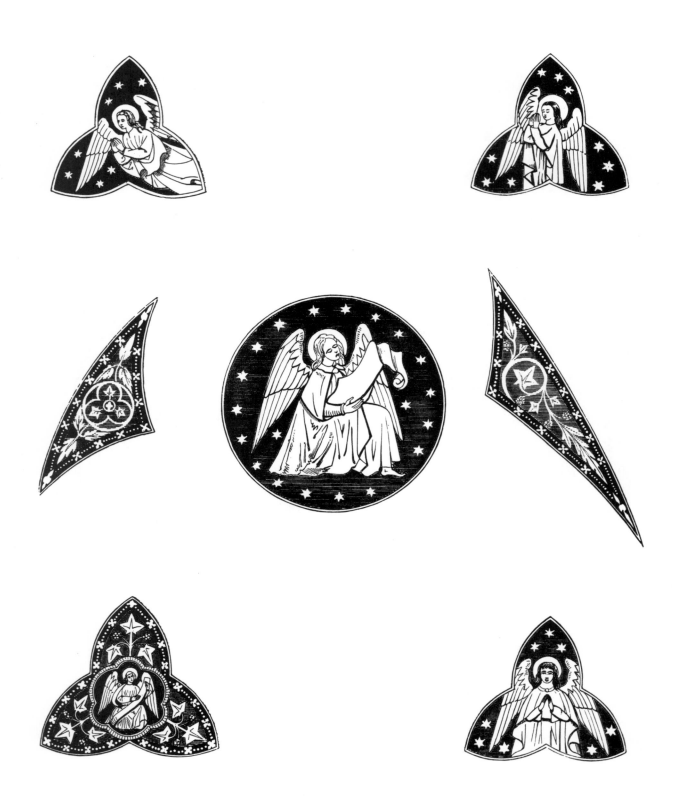

Trefoils and Spandrils, Ecclesiastical Windows

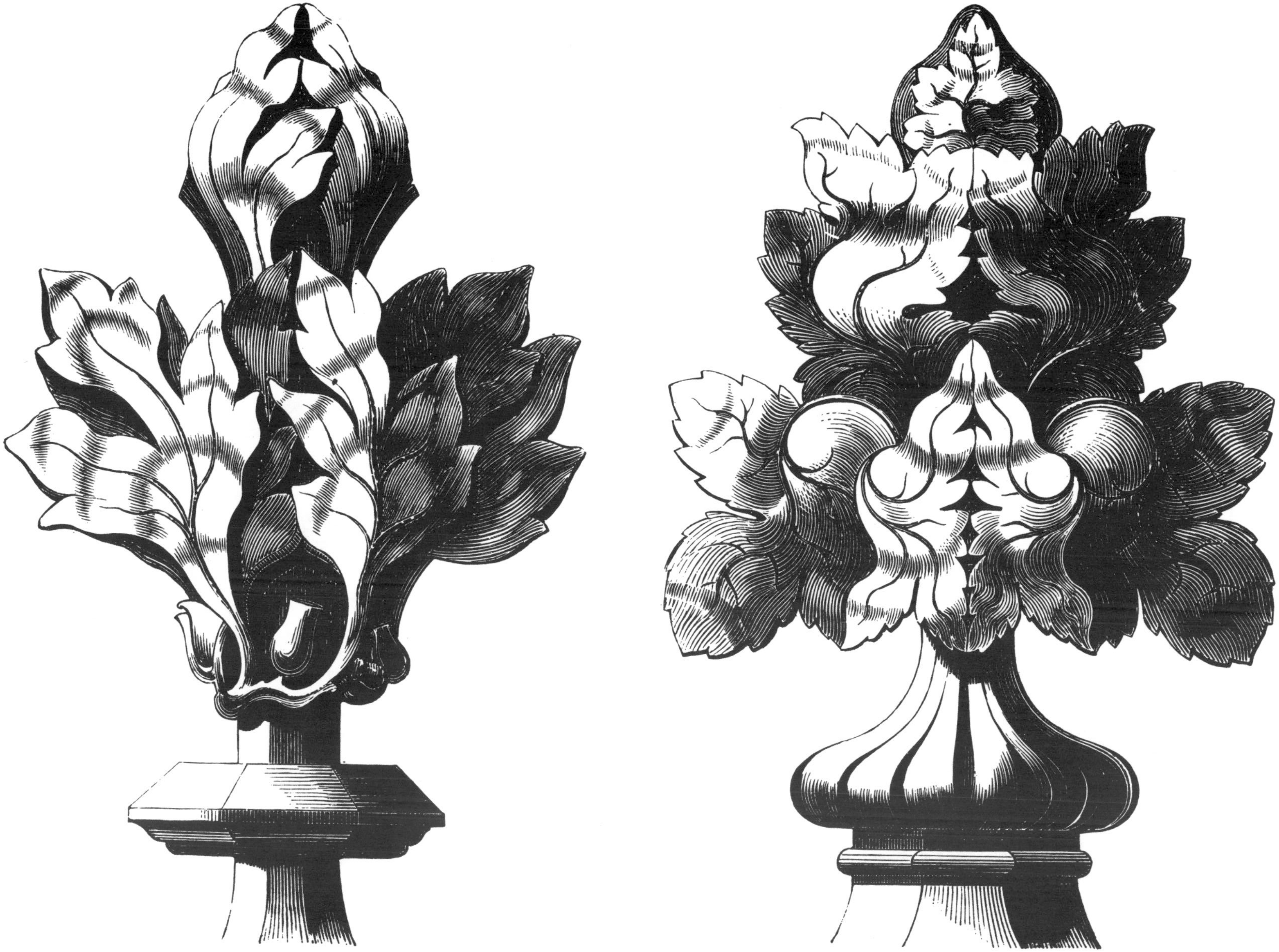

Decorated Gothic Finials

French Brackets and Italian Circular Ornament

Ceiling

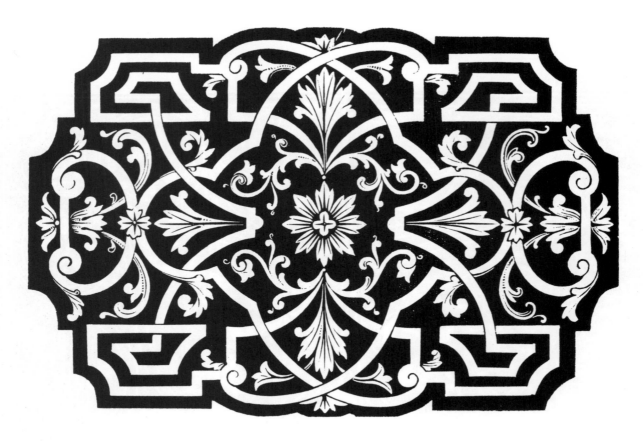

Arabesque Ceilings

Etruscan Ornament

Greek Ornaments